Conversations with Archangel Michael

Margaret Koester

Copyright © 2006 by Margaret Koester

All rights reserved. No part of this book shall be reproduced or transmitted in any form or by any means, electronic, mechanical, magnetic, photographic including photocopying, recording or by any information storage and retrieval system, without prior written permission of the publisher. No patent liability is assumed with respect to the use of the information contained herein. Although every precaution has been taken in the preparation of this book, the publisher and author assume no responsibility for errors or omissions. Neither is any liability assumed for damages resulting from the use of the information contained herein.

ISBN 0-7414-3492-X

Published by:

INFINITY
PUBLISHING.COM

1094 New DeHaven Street, Suite 100
West Conshohocken, PA 19428-2713
Info@buybooksontheweb.com
www.buybooksontheweb.com
Toll-free (877) BUY BOOK
Local Phone (610) 941-9999
Fax (610) 941-9959

Printed in the United States of America

Printed on Recycled Paper

Published November 2006

Table of Contents

Who is my source?..1
How did we come into being? 3
Does God know me?...5
By what name am I known? 8
What is the source of creativity?..9
What makes the world go round? 11
What is the reasoning behind the theory all men are
    created equal?..13
How can Lucifer create?...15
Who is the Holy Spirit? 16
Who is Jesus?..18
Who are angels?..20
Why do we have guardian angels? 22
What is the difference between life in body and life in
    spirit? 23
What do we do in spirit?...25
What does freedom mean?...27
Where are the seven realms, and what do they stand for?............29
What happens in purgatory and hell?..................................32
Is heaven a constant state of existence?..............................34
How can we interact on a spiritual level?............................35
How do thoughts come to be?..37
What is a Light form?...39
What is a vortex? 40
Why do we have bodies? 42
Is the world going through a cleansing?..............................44
What happened at The Last Supper?...................................46

Why are we here?	48
What is in it for me?	49
What is my part?	50
How can I change the world?	51
How can I make a difference?	52
How do people see me?	53
Can others count on me?	54
Where do my responsibilities begin and end in this world?	56
Why is the world filled with stress?	58
Why is everyone so restless?	60
Why do I feel like I am in a rut?	61
Why is life such a struggle?	62
What is the meaning of the saying "Life is Unfair"?	64
How can I live in the world but not of it?	65
Why do people do the things they do?	67
Why do people make a travesty of truth?	69
Why is it so hard for some people to know God?	70
Why is one person's belief system different from another person's belief system?	72
What is the "word of God"?	74
What are prayers?	75
What are principles of faith?	76
What are the seven deadly sins?	77
Who sets moral standards?	79
Why is there no mercy toward individuals who break the law?	80
How can differences in the matter of faith be reconciled?	83
How can I get answers?	85
How can I find an avenue to new ways of doing things?	87
How can I feel fulfilled?	89

What price do I pay for wanting more than God provides
 for my well-being?..90
What was everyday life like on earth before the fall? 92
What does everyday life mean?..94
How to live everyday life?..95
What is happiness? 97
What does it mean to live a life of fantasy?...............................99
What is meant by a sound mind in a sound body?....................101
What is disease?...103
How can I live a life of ease?...105
Why do bodies age?...107
How does a good gene become a bad gene in the process
 of heredity? 109
What are roads to recovery? 111
What is spiritual healing therapy? 113
What happens in decomposition of the body? 115
Will there ever be peace in the world?.....................................117
Is the world going through a cleansing? 118
Should people take it seriously when there is an
 earthquake? 120
What causes the earth to wobble?..121
Where is Atlantis?..123
Are we in "the end times"? 125
How could Jesus predict that 144,000 would rise in the
 rapture? 126
Are little children included in that number? 127
Will angels who have incarnated in body be part of the
 144,000?...128
Who is the anti-christ? 129
What is outer space and who is there?.....................................130

Who is my source?

Everything originates with The Source of All That Is, God. His thoughts for you are your thoughts, His sight for you is your sight, His words for you are your words, and His actions for you are your actions. But, with this, He also gives you free will to allow this to happen or to go your own way.

In letting God live through you, you are letting Him be who you are. He lives through each one of His creations this way, if allowed. It is one grand internet, far vaster than could ever be imagined by man. A person with questions can receive answers by asking others, all the while knowing that the answers are coming from God living through them. Complications set in when the people asked are ones who have gone their own way instead of allowing God to be who they are . . . and the answers are not always correct.

Guardian angels are available to fill in under the latter circumstance, when the words of others in the world cannot be trusted. This is how they keep a line of communication open between you and God. They are conduits for answers that God should be able to give you through other people.

But angels only answer questions of ones living good, gentle, kind and loving lives in everything they do or think or say. If ones questioning live other than lives of goodness, gentleness, kindness and Love, answers received come from other than angels and are not always reliable.

A life on earth can be lived in Oneness with God without reaching out to others for answers or talking with angels. And how that can be done is by living a life of goodness, gentleness, kindness and Love and allowing God to live through you in everything you do, or think, or say. That is, God's thoughts for you are your thoughts, God's sight for you is your sight, God's words for you are your words and God's actions for you are your actions.

How did we come into being?

First of all, there is what is called intelligence. Intelligence is. It has no beginning or end. It is eternal. Nothing exists outside of it. It is made up of light particles, compatible light particles that can coalesce spontaneously and result in creation.

It follows, then, that the one we know as the Creator can bring an idea to fulfillment through the coalescing of compatible light particles. The earth and the souls of earth were created in this way. When man creates, he brings compatible light particles together through a choice of components that he knows will coalesce to work together.

Everything that exists is part of the one intelligence. The compatible light particles brought together make the difference. On earth,

stones are:	mineral & water
plants:	mineral, water & inner growth
animals:	mineral, water, inner growth, sensation & movement
man:	mineral, water, inner growth, sensation & movement & consciousness.

As long as a creation remains in existence, it is "on line" with its Creator. The connection is at the core or heart area and we have the choice (free will) to stay on line or go our own way. While we are on line, we have the full benefits of intelligence. When we disconnect, we lose the full benefits and operate solely on an instinctual level, such as the animals do.

When we stay on line, or return after a period of disconnectedness, all thoughts that we experience are intelligent because their source is the intelligence of all. We need not "take thought," because it is all there for us. When we have an idea and follow through, the idea results in a creation that is part of the flow of intelligence.

When we disconnect, it is because our thoughts are incompatible with the thoughts of the intelligence, which are Love only. When other than loving thoughts are entertained, a separation occurs and man is on his own.

Does God know me?

Yes, and this is why.

Everything starts somehow, somewhere. You know that when you have an idea to make something, you look to see what you can put together to make that something. And you know it takes certain things. Not everything will go together to make what you want. You might say, the pieces have to fit together properly in order for your idea to work. And after you finish, you see that your idea is good and that it stands out as something different from anything else in the world.

This is how you came to be. You were someone's idea. And that someone is the one we call God. And what God has to draw on for what He wants to put together is Light particles. They are everywhere. But He knows it will take a certain kind. Not every Light particle will go together with another Light particle to make what He wants to make at the moment. They have to be ones that fit together properly if

His idea is to work. And after God finishes, He sees His idea as good and that it stands out as something different from anything else in all the universes.

Now, you may wonder why you cannot see God doing this. The reason is God made the world and the people on it a long time ago. He brought together the proper Light particles for each one. No two alike. All beautiful.

Then something happened that changed everything. The story involves an angel that God created . . . out of Light particles, the same way He creates everything else. This particular angel was not satisfied with life. He wanted more than God was providing for what he was doing. So, he fell out with God, and one of the things he did after that was come to the world where everything was beautiful, for the sole purpose of getting everyone on his side. His name is Lucifer. He told one named Adam not to be satisfied with what he had, that he could have more than God was providing for what he was doing. Adam fell for what Lucifer had to say. And that was his downfall, because we cannot have more than God provides for what we are doing no matter how hard we try. It is called being greedy. And when we are greedy, frustration sets in.

As Lucifer continued to talk to the people of the world, more and more went along with his way of thinking. Darkness settled over the land. Each person's Light form thickened into a body form. That is why when you look in a mirror, you see a body form instead of a Light form. But the body form still holds the Light form that was made by God out of Light particles. It lasts forever. It is the form you are in before you are born into the world in a body and the form you continue to be in after leaving a body when you die.

You may ask, "Why does a person want to be born into the world instead of staying in Light form only?" The answer is to reach out and save those who get caught up in the ways of the world and forget who they are. The only trouble is many that come to save get caught up in the ways of the world themselves.

This gives an understanding of why most people find themselves in the trouble they are in today. They have forgotten who they are and why they are here. They are lost. God knows you. God created you to live through you. So be and do, and let God be you. Let His thoughts for you be your thoughts. It will be at that time that you can turn to one who is lost, and then another and another, and tell them what you know. They will be saved.

By what name am I known?

You are known to your family and associates by the name given to you at birth. In spirit, you are known by your lights. A combination of the two is how you are known by your fellow human beings.

Trouble sets in when your lights become cloudy through association and a taking up with those of the world who have become lost and whose lights no longer shine. Your lights become entangled with theirs in a compromise that ends in your becoming lost to what you know to be true. A reassessment of your position in the world is in order.

Come to know who you are. You are a creation of God's. He created you to live through, but he can only live through you when your mind and his are compatible. God is Love only and He wants to live through you in that Love. It knows only gentleness and kindness. It does not know anger, avarice (greed), envy, gluttony, lust, pride or sloth.

What is the source of creativity?

Creativity is considered something out of the ordinary when it should be considered an everyday occurrence. Whenever you have an idea, where do you think it comes from? It comes from God, because God is you, and lives through you, as you.

This concept may be difficult for some to comprehend. Think of it this way. A creation needs a Creator: otherwise, we would not exist. A creation needs something out of which to be created. That something is the material or substance of all creation. It is Light, seen as light particles by those who have eyes to see. Everything created before, now or in the future is of this material or substance. Yes, people of earth are born of woman, but she, in cooperation with man, perpetuates creation . . . all out of the same material or substance.

Those of spirit are in a different form from what is comprehended by man as spirit. A body is a harder form of spirit. It is a body that is necessary for compatibility with conditions in the world. Spirits occupying stars and other planets exist in forms compatible with conditions in those places.

The Mind of God exists in all of His creations. It exists to the fullest extent in the minds of those who keep their thoughts compatible with His way of thinking. It is dimmer in the minds of those who do not keep their thoughts compatible with His way of thinking. All creative thinking comes from God's thoughts for you in the intention He has in creating you. Let your thinking be compatible with His way of thinking by being good and gentle, kind and loving and avoiding the seven deadly sins of anger, avarice (greed), envy, gluttony, lust, pride and sloth.

What makes the world go round?

The force that makes the world go round emanates from a star at the center of the twelve universes. The star was created by God. The force is called the God energy.

The God energy is tremendous. From the central star of the twelve universes, it flows through to the stars (suns) of each of the universes. It is in a constant pattern of motion, so that the universes and, in turn, their parts, do not collide. They have their pathways. In disk fashion, the world (Earth) revolves around the star or sun of the twelfth universe. In turn, and also in disk fashion, the star or sun of the twelfth universe, along with the stars or suns of the other eleven universes, revolves around the central star of the twelve universes.

The Earth is what is called a planet, and, along with planets Mercury, Venus, Mars, Jupiter, Saturn, Uranus, Neptune, Pluto, revolves around the sun of the twelfth universe. Each planet of a universe revolves in a left-to-right motion, so that each is in a constant circular motion of its own, along with a constant circular motion around the sun. The moons of planets revolve in a similar circular motion around each planet; however, they do not revolve in place as the planets do.

The order of the universes is maintained by the God energy, in this fashion.

And this is what makes the world go round.

What is the reasoning behind the theory all men are created equal?

Patterning is prevalent throughout the universes. A smooth flow would not exist otherwise. And the patterns are in the Mind of The Creator of All That Is. The patterns may be different, one from another, but only for the sake of variety. Otherwise, they are all equal in the eyes of The Creator.

Infused into each creation is the wherewithal to stay on course with the Creator; that is, the mind of the creation is at one with the Mind of The Creator. All is love, no other. If the mind of the creation entertains thoughts that are at variance with Love, a separation occurs. The mind of the creation is on its own.

A return to Love is all that is necessary to allow a reinfusion of one's mind with that of The Creator's. The Creator does not reach out, just waits. To return to the Love, it is necessary to be good, gentle, kind and loving and avoid the seven deadly sins. Then there is no longer a separation. All thoughts are on line again. Everything that is in need of being known is known.

How can Lucifer create?

You may ask how Lucifer can create things that are not of God, when God's Light is everywhere.

God's radiance is everywhere. And distortions of it coexist with the pure Light. God's radiance is available to everyone to do with it what they would. Some stay in the pure Light and some distort it by their thinking. They make it something it is not. An example would be people distorting Truth. Truth and non-truth coexist, but non-truth is on its own. It exists in the minds of those who believe in it, but it is not part of God.

Just remember, everyone has free will to do what he or she pleases with God's radiance, but God is only present in that which remains in His Love.

Who is the Holy Spirit?

The energy that emanates from God is the Holy Spirit (holy meaning whole). It encompasses and lives through all of God's creations. Life could not be without it.

When a soul or angel's body dies to life on earth, the spirit that enlivened it lives on and may, if desired, be born into body many times. This is not reincarnation. It is incarnating again and again. The spirit of a soul or angel lives on because it is in a state of consciousness. When the body of a plant, animal, fish, bird dies, the spirit returns to a formless state of light particles only. Nevertheless, this should not be hastened, as happens so many times. Things created by the fallen angels like pests, weeds, spiders, bugs, etc. (to annoy man) also return to a formless state when they die. It will not matter if their deaths are hastened.

If, at some point, a soul or angel born into a body forgets who he or she is and constantly defies God, lifetime after lifetime, a return to a formless state of light particles can be an eventuality.

Who is Jesus?

Jesus is an angel, known in spirit as Jesias. He is an angel created by God, and dwells with God at the Source or what is sometimes referred to as the Godhead. The Godhead consists of one star or sun. It is the Light of this sun that God sent into the world. And this is one thing that is misunderstood. When God created Jesias, His intention for Him was there in what might be called a blueprint. God, in creating all that exists: angels, humans, etc., stamps each with His intention, or blueprint. God focuses His Light through His creations, including angels. And when Jesus was born into the world, God focused His Light through Him. It was a magnitude of Light that was possible because of God's intention for Him when He created Him.

There is much controversy in the world today about the role Jesus played. Jesus brought messages of Truth; a Truth perpetuated by those who believe. It was not His intention that churches form around His teachings. He brought His teachings for everyone, teachings to be taught at a mother's knee, you might say, rather than involving going to a certain church and listening to a certain teacher. It is not necessary to have churches or a fine array of clothing and furnishings for the teaching of Truth. Those who live in the Love and Light of God and understand Truth can teach it to others. In the beginning of the world, there were no religions, no churches, synagogues or meeting places for the teaching of Truth. Everyone knew Truth. It was only after the fall that many, who thought they were remaining in the Light, taught those they felt had separated from the Light. This was the start of churches.

Who are angels?

They may not be who you think they are. They do not have faces. They do not have bodies. They are ideas of God's.

In the beginning, when the world was new, everyone understood this about themselves. It was only after man separated himself from the God consciousness that he had to have a housing for his consciousness. And angels, in appearing to man, took on dimensions that man could recognize.

To make this more understandable: when God creates, it is His idea that comes into being. And the creation holds its form as long as God holds the idea. Everyone has an energy field with a heart at the center. It is through the heart that God communicates with and through you. It is a spiritual heart, a focus of Light, at the juncture of two crossing beams of Light.

Everyone is recognized in spirit by his Light. Each is different in some way, in the same way that humans have different faces. Faces came into being as man could no longer see in the Light. A face is what man sees, but it is the Light within a person that makes the person recognizable in spirit for who he or she is. That is the foundation for the saying, "By his Light you shall know him."

12

Why do we have guardian angels?

Guardian angels are angels assigned by God to guard the link of energy He has with each of his creations on earth. Before the fall, the spirits, or souls of earth, did not need guardian angels. It was after the fall, when man separated his mind from the Mind of God, that God assigned angels.

You may wonder why guardian angels are necessary. They are necessary because a spirit in body does not always maintain the link he has with God. There are too many distractions in the world; distractions that continue to be perpetrated by those who have followed a separate thinking process . . . the one generated by the fall of Adam. Your guardian angel maintains the link for you.

When you are alone sometime, speak to your guardian angel. You will receive a reply when you and your guardian angel join in one mind in the Mind of God. Voices heard up to that point may be less than desirable.

What is the difference between life in body and life in spirit?

God creates with the intention of living through each of His creations. And as he lives through each of His creations, with thoughts for each, an influence of one to another prevails. All is bliss.

When a soul is in a state of bliss, either in spirit form or in body form, no thought is taken as to what to do next. The soul lets go and lets God's thoughts for him be his thoughts. In spirit, the result is in spirit form; in body, the result is in material form. God created the world and its inhabitants in spirit so that they could join with Him in His grand mosaic of Love, their intention and influence throughout the universes being one of charity. Only a discordant thought could make a difference. The fall of man and what followed derailed the intention and influence.

From that time on, man lived in either spirit form or body

form. When in spirit, a soul of earth has a bigger picture of creation than he has while in body. He understands creation and God's role in it. He understands his role. If he has lived in the Love while in body, he had no problem making the transition to spirit only. He takes up where he left off. If he has not lived in the Love while in body, he relearns what he forgot. In other words, he goes back to school. The angels teach him what is necessary to return to a state of bliss.

What do we do in spirit?

Life in spirit is a lot like life on earth, or life on any of the stars and planets, except that time is not separated into day and night or into seasons of the year. And there is no need for sleep. But, there is activity, and the props used in the process are the same as the props used by humans, except that they are in spirit only. God lives through His creations with the intentions He has for them, whether in spirit or body. Wherever a creation of God's is located in the vast universes, a link is maintained, one heart to another, to God and each other. All is part of the evolutionary process.

Life in spirit differs from life in body in only one respect, and that is in intelligence. In spirit, an entity has access to the overall intelligence of God, the Source of All That Is. Souls of earth had this access before the fall, but now it is limited to those of earth who have come to an understanding of who they are and allow themselves to be part of the intelligence.

Souls in spirit live on seven planes of enlightenment, while going through a re-indoctrination into the Truth they lost while living in body. Earthbound souls in spirit live apart from the rest, but at any time of their choice they can proceed to the seven planes of enlightenment. They are what are usually referred to as lost souls.

Souls of the seven planes who incarnate do so from the 7th, the one often referred to as 7th Heaven, the sole purpose being to enlighten souls of earth to Truth. Earthbound souls incarnate from their own level, without a re-indoctrination into Truth. In body, as well as in spirit, they can, at any time, allow themselves to be enlightened to Truth.

15

What does freedom mean?

The word 'free' is looked on as meaning 'no obligation, no strings attached.' When something is free, it holds a special place in its appeal. No one is beholden. No one need feel obligated in any way.

When God created man, he instilled in him free will, a freedom to stay in His Love or to go his own way. All was in spirit. But, as a result of Lucifer's visit to the Garden of Eden and his tempting of Adam to want more than God was providing for what he was doing, man made his first choice as a free man. He chose greed. He chose to want more than God was providing for what he was doing. As a result, he was out of the Love and dead to God. A hardening of spirit provided a body in which to get around in his separated state.

Man did not lose free will. He has every opportunity to return to God in His Love. All he need do is live a good, gentle, kind and loving life and avoid the seven deadly sins of anger, avarice (greed), envy, gluttony, lust, pride and sloth.

16

Where are the seven realms, and what do they stand for?

The realms start beyond earth's magnetism. They are:

Earthbound. Souls who are earthbound had a choice, when leaving body, between going to the Light or remaining earthbound. They chose to remain earthbound, and are in a hell of their own making. The warmth of God's Love reaches them, but it feels intense because they have not lived in God's Love while on earth. The choice is always open for them to turn to the Love and rise to higher realms. Evil spirits are being held in check at this time, but earthbound spirits can enter bodies of ones who allow themselves to be open to possession.

1st Souls of the first realm are souls who have grossly malfunctioned in a world of their own making, completely devoid of an understanding of who they are and the impact of their actions on others. This realm is known as purgatory.

The purging comes in the Love of God. Where God is, there can be no other.

2nd Souls of the second realm are souls who have had no understanding of who they are. They are occupied with doing things that bring them closer to the understanding of who they are.

3rd Souls of the third realm have reached the point where they understand there is a God, and that God created them. They are occupied with doing things that bring them closer to the understanding of what is implied.

4th Souls of the fourth realm have reached the point where they understand that every thought, word and deed in the physical was at variance with being One with God. They are occupied with doing things that bring them closer to the understanding of what they did in life that kept them from being One with God.

5th Souls of the fifth realm have reached the point where they understand that their thoughts are at variance with the thoughts of God, or the One Mind. They are occupied with doing things that bring them closer to an understanding of what thoughts they need to let go of, in order to be of One mind with God.

6th Souls of the sixth realm have reached the point where they understand what it means to be One with God, but have not practiced it. They are occupied with doing things that bring them closer to an understanding of the need to practice what it means to be One with God.

7th Souls of the seventh realm have reached the point where they are One with God. They are occupied with doing those things that demonstrate to the souls of lower realms what it means to be One with God.

Souls who return directly to the seventh realm are ones who have been good, gentle, kind and loving while on earth and have avoided the seven deadly sins of anger, avarice (greed), envy, gluttony, lust, pride and sloth.

17

What happens in purgatory and hell?

Purgatory

Purgatory is the meeting ground between soul in body and soul in spirit. When a soul leaves this plane, it is in a bright Light, and during this time, loved ones in spirit come to greet the person. At a much later time, after soul-searching is complete, the person is taken to an area compatible with his or her level of consciousness. For those who had difficulty in life in coming to the realization of a Oneness with God, time is taken to explain it clearly until it is thoroughly understood. This is purgatory. There is a purging of preconceived ideas about Reality and Truth. After this period of time, a person is taken to a higher level of consciousness where learning continues.

Hell

There is one difference between purgatory and hell. When the soul searching is complete, those who are pure of heart, but have not recognized their Oneness with God, go to purgatory. Those who are not pure of heart, go to a place reserved for those who are insistent on defying God. Making mistakes in this world are forgiven by God, but not defiance of His Power . . . a wanting to replace him in what they do. Contrary to what is said in churches, souls can eventually leave hell when they are willing to no longer defy God. They go through the learning process from purgatory on. They are aware that this is what is necessary for freedom.

Purgatory and Hell

Both purgatory and hell are filled with God's Love, the same as in the consciousness called heaven. Those who are defiant and those who have not recognized their Oneness with God are filled with this Love to the intensity of purification that is needed. And this is what is uncomfortable.

18

Is heaven a constant state of existence?

Heaven is. It is all encompassing. There is nothing that is not heaven. It is God's world. It is Love.

Those who live a life of Love are conscious of their heavenly existence. Those who do not are not conscious of it. When they were born into the world, they were, but as time went by and they were caught up in the ways of the world, they became lost. They ended up on their own, in a life of their own making.

Heavenly consciousness encompasses the minds of all who exist. All minds are as One. All minds are all-knowing. Those who live a life of Love live in this state of mind all the time. Those who do not are lost. They are on their own, in a mind of their own making.

19

How can we interact on a spiritual level?

Actually, all life is on a spiritual level. It was divided, in man's mind, after the fall. When man's mind was separated from the One Mind of God, it was felt, thereafter, that spiritual interaction was on two levels. What really happened is the mind of the soul became divided into limited and unlimited thinking.

The mind is unlimited when a soul lives a life whereby he or she is good, gentle, kind and loving and does not entertain the seven deadly sins of anger, avarice (greed), envy, gluttony, lust, pride and sloth. When this happens, the soul's mind and God's mind are as One. No separation. All a person needs to function in the world is available, body, mind and spirit. The interaction is on a mental level. All thoughts needed 'cross the person's mind.' You will hear a person say, "A thought just crossed my mind, etc." These thoughts can be counted on. If a thought is not present at a certain time, it is because a thought is not necessary, regarding a situation, at a certain time.

The mind is limited when a soul lives a life whereby he or she is not good, gentle, kind and loving and entertains the seven deadly sins of anger, avarice (greed), envy, gluttony, lust, pride and sloth. It is dead to the Mind of God, meaning there is no interaction with the Mind of God. Thoughts that come are from ego. The person is on his or her own.

20

How do thoughts come to be?

Thoughts originate in the brain. They arrive there through a process called intuition. In other words, you intuit thoughts.

Thoughts and the eyes are as one. This may be hard to believe, but it is true. Without the eyes, thoughts originate in the mind, but not through the process of intuition. They originate through stimulus of the senses.

Intuition and the stimulus of the senses come about on two different nerve tracts to the brain. Intuition originates along nerve tracts that connect the eyes to the brain. Stimulus of the senses originates along nerve tracts that connect the senses to the brain.

Thoughts are things, the same way a table is a table; a lamp is a lamp, etc. The expression of them is another matter. They are expressed in languages, handed down from generation to generation, in various parts of the world. A thought does not lose its meaning, although described in several different languages.

"But," you may ask, "what are the processes of intuition and the stimulus of the senses that form thoughts or things in the brain?" The thoughts or things that form in the brain are impressions seen with the eyes or felt with the senses. There are no words to describe them.

21

What is a Light form?

A Light form is a segment of energy that surrounds an idea before it enters the brain. It is sent by God. Most people do not see it beforehand. Only those sensitive to spirit.

God's thoughts for a person in the Light are continuous and do not present themselves as separate Light forms. It is only when a person is not living in Oneness with God and God wants to present an idea to the person that he uses this method of transference of thought.

22

What is a vortex?

A vortex is a void. It is space between. In creation, light particles coalesce or are coalesced as a form for an idea. Around creations, in between creations is a void, a vortex. It consists of light particles ever present, ever ready to be coalesced into a creation. An earthly example is in the building of a house and then the building of another house. There is space between them. It is a void or a vortex. It is not without energy. It is just that a creation does not exist that uses the energy at the moment.

There are vortexes everywhere. When one is noticed, it is taken as a big event. But energy noticed in moving through a vortex feels different only because it is different from the energy in so-called solid objects around it.

A vortex is not to be confused with what is called a pocket of energy. That is different. It is when the atmosphere shifts from being mostly sunny to mostly cloudy, etc. and sets up various intensities or pockets of energy in the atmosphere. The airlines call it turbulence.

23

Why do we have bodies?

When the world was new, there were no bodies . . . only spirit. As time went by and man turned away from God, due to the fall, bodies started to form. It was a hardening process, due to hardening of spirit.

Also, in the process, everything started to harden in order to adapt to this new mode of life. That is the reason things around you are of a dense nature. Eventually, all within view of man became visible to him, as the need arose. At first, he could not see the planets. Then, as his vision adjusted, he could see them. All stars and planets, except the world, are in spirit only. All inhabitants of other planets are in spirit only.

You may wonder how this can be if you see them. When man first developed a body, he could not see things of a spirit nature, but ever so gradually, things started to come into his line of vision. Not all, only what was necessary for him to see. Things of a spirit nature are available to man to see when he has the eyes to see them. This is happening more every day. An example in recent years is seeing, for the first time, the planets Neptune and Pluto. They were called discoveries, but they were always there, being created before the world.

The Moon has a different history, even though created during the same time frame as the world. The sole purpose of the Moon is to shine reflective Light from the Sun when parts of the world are not in direct line with the Sun's rays.

24

Is the world going through a cleansing?

Something is going on all over the world, and it is a puzzle to its inhabitants. The phenomenon is not an environmental problem, as many suppose. It is much more. It is a world cleansing.

The world has reached that stage in its existence when it needs a monumental bath. Filth is piling up, out of all proportions. Wars have left debris over most of the earth, in one form or another, above and below ground. Pollutants have filled the atmosphere until very little clean air exists.

Cleansing of the world started around 2,000 years ago. It was a time when an alignment of the stars and planets let the Light from the Godhead, or Source of all things, reach earth in its fullest intensity. The Light has been cleansing earth of impurities ever since, and will continue to do so until further realignment of the stars and planets.

Peaking of the Light will take place around 2011. By then, impurities will be gone. The earth will be pure again. Then the Light will wane. Once before, in the existence of the world, a cleansing took place. It was at the time of the great flood, when dinosaurs disappeared from the face of the earth.

25

What happened at The Last Supper?

The supper that is usually referred to as The Last Supper involved a gathering of Jesus and his twelve apostles, the ones He had assigned to spread His word to the multitudes. It was not intended to be His last supper with them. Circumstances intervened that ended His life on earth.

During the last supper, and as He had done on other occasions, Jesus spoke to the apostles on ways to enlighten people about their return to a state of being of One Mind with The Mind of God. God lives through all of His creations, including the mind. His thoughts are His creations' thoughts. But He gives everyone free will, and if they deign not to be of One Mind with Him, they are on their own and their thoughts are not His thoughts for them. To stay of One Mind with God, it is necessary to be gentle, kind and loving and avoid the seven deadly sins of anger, avarice (greed), envy, gluttony lust, pride and sloth. God knows only Love.

During the supper, Jesus explained to His followers that God's light is everywhere, even in a piece of bread. He broke His bread and handed out a piece to each apostle. They ate the bread as Jesus said, "Take and do likewise." The bread has become a wafer, but it is still symbolic and a reminder of the existence of God's Light being everywhere.

26

Why are we here?

We are here on earth on a mission to encourage everyone to stay of One Mind with God. We do this by first making sure our own thinking is aligned with His, and then becoming living examples of who God is.

God's design for us includes free will: a decision to stay of One Mind with Him; that is, keeping our thoughts in line with His thoughts or to live in a separated state by entertaining thoughts that are incompatible with His.

When we stay of One Mind with God in his Love, we experience a life of love, joy, peace and prosperity. When we live in a separated state, we experience a life of fear, hate, cruelty and sadness.

27

What is in it for me?

Compensation is a way of life in the world. Most everyone expects gratification of some kind or another for a job well done. It seems as though a thank-you note does not always suffice.

Working for a living and expecting remuneration is one thing. A livelihood depends on it. But expecting something in return for every little thing that one does for another borders on greed. Goodwill ends up as a commodity.

Reach out to those in need. See where you can make a difference. If 'What is in it for me?' crosses your mind, remember compensation can be a warm feeling in the heart for a job well done.

28

What is my part?

Souls were created by God at the same time he created the world. They are what are known as eternal souls.

It was intended that the souls would live in a state of bliss in Oneness with God. The fall of man changed that. Bodies formed to house the souls who lived in a separated state. Ever since, souls have been incarnating to reach those of a separated state to bring them back to God.

God influences through all of his creations, throughout all the universes, including the Sun, Moon and planets of the earth's solar system. Souls of earth, of their own volition (free will), enter bodies at times that the influences of the Sun, Moon and planets are in an alignment most suitable to what they would like to do while here. It does not matter what souls do in the world as far as jobs are concerned, as long as the jobs allow time for them to reach and redirect souls who forgot the reason why they are here on earth.

29

How can I change the world?

By, first of all, changing yourself. A few, but very few, live a life that allows them to make a difference in the world. Most do not. Be one of the ones who make a difference.

Start by realizing your attunement to spirit. You came into the world in complete attunement. Then, gradually, ever so gradually, you got caught up in a lifestyle of those who had fallen into a world of their own making. They forgot who they were and wander in a world of illusion.

To have a clear vision of the world and your place in it, return to the simple life of the child that you were before your mind became contaminated with falsehoods. Be good, gentle, kind and loving and avoid the seven deadly sins of anger, avarice (greed), envy, gluttony, lust, pride and sloth. Your mind will clear and you will be living a life of attunement to spirit. Your mind will be as One with the Mind of God, your Creator.

30

How can I make a difference?

Each soul of earth and each angel of the universes is different, because God created them individually, with certain attributes He wanted them to have. In other words, each fills a slot of intention.

Not everyone remembers his or her intention, because of being caught up in the ways of the world and going along with what everyone else says. This leaves a void. What the person was to do in the world is left undone. To make a difference in the world, one only needs to be aware of God's intention and fulfill it.

The way to know God's intention for you is to listen to your heart. In other words, ask yourself "What do I have my heart in doing?" Listen closely. Be aware. You will know what it is you would really love to do. And when you know, start putting it into motion. In this way, you will make a difference.

31

How do people see me?

Everyone is seen in a different light. To one person, you may be seen in name only. To another, by a service rendered. No matter how, in one way or another, you are invariably stamped in the memory of all those who enter your life.

You may ask, 'Do people see me as I see and know myself to be or do they see me in another way?' Sometimes, other people see and know you better than you see and know yourself. You may wonder how that can be. Truth will out. No matter how much you try to hide your true self, it will always show.

See yourself as good, gentle, kind and loving and one who avoids the seven deadly sins and you will know that others see and know you as you see and know yourself to be.

32

Can others count on me?

Counting on others is the way people describe faith in others. If you can count on someone, that someone is reliable. The moment that person fails in one way or another, he or she is considered no longer reliable. You cannot count on the person.

Have you ever stopped to think how important it is to others that they can count on you? Be the person who is reliable. It makes such a big difference in other people's lives. They know that at least one other person is there for them. They trust.

How many people are there in the world that you can trust? Not many. The result is a loss of faith in life, a loss of faith in the very support you need for your existence in the world. You feel lost.

This describes the present state of the world. Very few have faith in government, the banking system, the educational system, the medical field, and often the very ones who tell them about God.

You may ask, "What can I do about it?" Be a person others can trust, can count on, have faith in. Be a port in a storm.

33

Where do my responsibilities begin and end in this world?

The biggest responsibility people have in this world is to conduct themselves in a way that allows God to live through them and reach out to others. They can do this by being a good example; that is, by being good, gentle, kind and loving and avoiding the seven deadly sins.

Reaching out a helping hand is a responsibility. This can be done personally, by donating to a worthy cause or by supporting organizations that see to the less fortunate.

Seeing to it that children are treated well is a responsibility. They should be given a chance to grow up as healthy citizens of the world, knowing right from wrong, and how to pass it on to following generations.

And last, but not least, treating those close to you with love and affection is a responsibility. In this way, they feel good about themselves, pass it along to others and, in so doing, spread cheer and goodwill throughout the world.

34

Why is the world filled with stress?

It wasn't always that way. When the world was new, everything was spirit. The world was spirit. Inhabitants were spirit. And all were in close association with the angels. It was beautiful. Everything went along as a matter of course. Everyone loved everyone else. Everyone knew their oneness with God and His intentions for them. And they knew that God met all their needs so intentions could be fulfilled.

It would have remained that way, but one was tempted by Lucifer to desire more than God supplied him. The one is known as Adam. He succumbed. This threw everything off balance. There could no longer be peace and love and harmony. Man strived for more than God supplied for what he was doing. In defiance, he fell away from Oneness with God. He defied the natural order of things. And this caused disruption. It was the start of stress, which resulted in disease of the mind and then disease of the body. Contact with

God became less and less the more and more that God's creations, in their striving, separated themselves from Him. He could no longer live through them. His Light dimmed, and they were alone in the world.

God assigned guardian angels to guide them back to Him. The intent was to help them understand that their frustrations were because of an unnatural state of affairs. They no longer had access to the great Mind of God, or the energy that was theirs if they wanted it. They functioned in their separate minds. This has gone on for eons of time until the world has reached a state where there are very few who have remained in the Light of God. It behooves man to let go of his worldly ways and return to his natural state, and that is Oneness with God in the Love and Light that hold His wisdom.

35

Why is everyone so restless?

Before the fall, everyone in the world knew why they were here and what they came to do. They were content. There was no wondering what to do next. They knew.

After the fall, however, everything was different. Gone was the state of mind that was one with God's Mind. Everyone started to think for himself. The world was no longer the world God had planned. Bodies formed to house the spirits of separate mind. Restlessness set in. Roaming the world became the thing to do . . . always in search of what was missing since man's mind became separate from God's Mind. They were no longer content. They wondered what to do next. They didn't know.

Ever since the fall, spirits, including angels, have entered bodies in the world to try to return them to a state of one-mindedness. To no avail. Most people still wander here and there trying to find themselves.

36

Why do I feel like I am in a rut?

Landing in a rut is an awakening. It is a sign that you have not been pursuing a lifestyle that is consistent with God's intention for you in this world. God's intention for you is embedded in your heart. To get out of a rut, ask the question, 'What do I have my heart in doing? And listen for the answer. It will be there.

Lifestyles vary, one from another. What one person feels comfortable in doing, another may feel very uncomfortable in doing. Look around. Look for what you know in your heart you would feel comfortable in doing. Pursue it.

Finding your niche in the world is important. One of the pathways of life is filled that would, otherwise, be left unfilled. You feel fulfilled where otherwise you would feel unfulfilled. You are no longer in a rut.

37

Why is life such a struggle?

Life is a struggle because of problems dating as far back as the fall. There were no problems before that event. Life was beautiful. Ever since, life has gradually eroded until it is barely recognizable for what it was intended to be.

Before the fall, man was of One Mind with God. His thoughts were God's thoughts for him. He did not have to think of what to do next. The thought was there for him. That was all well and good until Lucifer, the fallen angel, introduced a new way of thinking. It led man astray. He introduced the thought that man should ask God for more than God was providing for what he was doing. This led to a separation of man's mind from the Mind of God. Man was on his own. Life became a struggle.

To get rid of the struggle, man needs to turn his life around and live a simple one of goodness, gentleness, kindness and Love. That is the way it was before the fall. When man left these attributes behind, he moved into a world of anger, avarice (greed), envy, gluttony, lust, pride and sloth . . . . a world of his own doing, a world of struggle.

38

What is the meaning of the saying "Life is Unfair"?

Life is looked on as fair or unfair according to how a person sees it. It is considered fair when all is going well and unfair when it is not. Not many understand that life is what you make it.

Life lived in a way that is satisfying to one person is considered fair. Life lived in a way that is unsatisfying or dissatisfying to another is considered unfair. Satisfaction is elusive because what satisfies one person may dissatisfy another.

The key to a life that is fair and satisfying is available to all. Look to what you have your heart in doing. Therein lies the key.

39

How can I live in the world but not of it?

How to live in the world but not of it requires an understanding of who you are. You are a spirit with a body. When the world was new and all was spirit only, it was easy to live in the world. All were one with God, in His Love. Everyone was good, gentle, kind and loving and did not know of the seven deadly sins of anger, avarice (greed), envy, gluttony, lust, pride, and sloth.

It was after the fall, when Lucifer tempted Adam to want more than God was providing for him, that the situation changed. Bodies formed. The souls who stayed faithful to God, content with what He was providing for them, were in body, but, upon leaving it, returned to the Light. Later, if they so wished, they could, and still do, enter bodies of newborns to do what they can, through them, to turn the world around to the Light. They are living in the world, but not of it.

The souls who fell away in discontent with what God was providing for them also had bodies, but, upon leaving them, remained earthbound in spirit. They did not go to the Light. They possessed, and still do, souls of those who turn away from God's love. They are living in the world and of it, as it is since the fall.

40

Why do people do the things they do?

People do the things they do, because they feel moved to. And that is the way it should be. The only thing is they are not always moved by God. In some cases, what they do originates from a mind that is separate from the Mind of God. Somewhere along the line, they took on thoughts that were at variance with God's thoughts of Love. In other instances, they went so far as to allow themselves to be open to possession by an earthbound spirit. In still other instances, they were influenced by family members or associates. In any case, God could no longer live through them.

However, God does not desert those who go off on their own. As in the story of the prodigal son, he waits for their return. The return is simple. All one need do is be good, gentle, kind and loving and avoid the seven deadly sins of anger, avarice (greed), envy, gluttony, lust, pride, sloth. The return is immediate.

From that moment on, the mind is one with the Mind of God in His Love. And all that one feels moved to do will have originated from that source. It is often referred to as 'the knowing.'

41

Why do people make a travesty of truth?

People make a travesty of Truth for many reasons. First, there is the lack of understanding of what Truth is. For instance, they may believe in God, but have no idea God is living through them. They may believe in the supernatural, but have no idea they are part of it. They may believe in life after death, but have no idea they continue to live on in spirit after death of the body.

You may ask, "How do I know if something is Truth?" You will know Truth if it holds up to 'the light of day;' in other words, if it remains Truth no matter which way you look at it. You will know Truth by the way you feel. It will always feel good to you. Truth never lets you down. It is constant; that is, non-changing, fickle or wavering.

Truth is the way things are. It cannot be glossed over. It will always remain Truth in spite of what people do, think, or say to make it otherwise. It makes sense. It is real. It is unfailing.

42

Why is it so hard for some people to know God?

Down through the ages, God has been mentioned over and over again, but is dismissed by many as mythical, meaning only a story that has been handed down from one generation to another. Little do they know that, in actuality, they would not exist only for the Spirit of God being their very being.

God is at the center of all the universes. He gave birth to all the stars and planets and life thereon, as an extension of Himself. He lives through them. There is no separation, but there is free will. Each creation can choose to stay of One Mind with God or go its own way. If a creation stays of One Mind with God, the benefits are tremendous. God is Love only and the creation is Love only. But if the creation chooses to go its own way, it becomes lost because it does not have the Love to sustain it. It lives in a void and grapples with life as best it can, on its own, with no loving support.

Living a life of goodness, gentleness, kindness and Love and avoiding the seven deadly sins of anger, avarice (greed), envy, gluttony, lust, pride and sloth affords one a closeness to God in His Love. The seven deadly sins are called deadly because the one who entertains them is dead to God.

43

Why is one person's belief system different from another person's belief system?

In the beginning, all souls of earth had a common belief system. It was simple. They believed God created them as models of Himself. They believed God created them with a purpose for being. They believed God created them with free will to stay as one with Him in common thought or go their own way.

Trouble set in when souls were influenced by the fallen angel Lucifer to want more than God was providing for what they were doing. Gone was the thought that they were created as models of God. Gone was the belief that God created them with a purpose for being. Gone was the belief that God created them with free will to stay as one with Him in common thought.

Souls became lost. They lost their connection with God. They were on their own. Ever since they have been trying to come up with a common belief system like they had before. Jesus tried to return common thought, but not all would believe Him. But enough have to keep the resurgence alive. Would that all would follow His example in the return of all souls of earth to a common belief system.

44

What is the "word of God"?

The "word of God" is misunderstood. It is often thought that words from outer space direct us from outside ourselves. The word of God comes from within. God creates to live through His creations in every thought, word and deed.

God lives through all those who live compatible with His way of thinking and that is being good, gentle, kind and loving and avoiding the seven deadly sins. That is being of one mind with God. Otherwise, He waits for their return.

To live in the world on one's own is like living without a rudder. There is no connection to the One Mind. A person is on his or her own, without a knowing as to how to think or what to do in the world. The person is lost.

Stay close to God. Think along the same lines. You will no longer be lost. You will be safe in the knowing that God lives through you with the thoughts He has for you.

45

What are prayers?

Prayers are petitions. Prayers are asking God for more than He has already provided for a lifetime experience. They are unnecessary. Instead of praying, a person should listen to his or her heart for answers.

When God creates a soul or angel, He has an intention in mind, and, along with the intention, the wherewithal to fulfill the intention. It is on a spiritual disk in the heart area. If a person lives in a way that allows this to happen, life goes smoothly. But, if a person takes his or her own head about life, ignoring what comes from the heart, ego sets in and life is downhill from there on in. The person is lost.

To get back on track, where what is known in the heart is known in the head, it is necessary for a person to be good, gentle, kind and loving and avoid the seven deadly sins. It may be an effort to do this at first, but, in time, it can become as natural as eating and sleeping.

46

What are principles of faith?

Each religious persuasion adopts what it believes to be its principles of faith, the tapestry of which is woven by those who adhere to a common viewpoint on matters of spirituality. Faith is an undying commitment to what is held to be true. Since there are so many principles of faith in the numerous religious persuasions in the world and no two alike, the question is "Which one holds truth? And if God created souls and angels to live through, how can He be of more than one mind on matters of faith and be true to Himself?

Before the fall, all were of one faith. After the fall, minds were splintered into numerous faiths. A return to simplicity of faith is necessary for all to return to the oneness of God. It is goodness, gentleness, kindness and love and a renouncing of the seven deadly (dead to God) sins of anger, avarice (greed), envy, gluttony, lust, pride and sloth. God is only Love.

47

What are the seven deadly sins?

Anger: Anger is asserting oneself, at the expense of another, to forcibly get a point across.

Avarice: Avarice is greed. It is wanting more than what is needed for what one is doing.

Envy: Envy is thinking that another person's self-worth is better than one's own self-worth.

Gluttony: Gluttony is gobbling everything in sight without taking others into consideration.

Lust: Lust is misuse of sexual urges.

Pride: Pride is thinking of one's self-worth as better than another person's self-worth.

Sloth: Sloth is laziness. It is a stifling of God's intention.

Jesus is the one who brought the deadly sins to the attention of the populace, by explaining to them that when one entertains one or more of the sins, he or she is dead to God. God can no longer live through someone who entertains thoughts that are adverse to His way of thinking, which is Love.

48

Who sets moral standards?

God sets moral standards. They are integral to the creative process. They are at the very core of existence. Without them, life is less than whole and eventually disintegrates.

The world is gradually disintegrating because of a lack of morals. The very fiber of its being is giving way. And it is because of a moral decline in its inhabitants. The whole is the sum of its parts, and since the inhabitants of the world are part of the whole, they affect the state of the world in general.

A return to moral standards is imperative to the well-being of the world. Set an example by being good, gentle, kind and loving and avoiding the seven deadly sins of anger, avarice (greed), envy, gluttony, lust, pride and sloth.

49

Why is there no mercy toward individuals who break the law?

There is the law of the land and the law of spirit. The law of the land is to respect other people and their property. The law of spirit is the Ten Commandments. They are recorded as given by God to Moses:

I am the Lord thy God. Thou shalt not bear false witness against me.

Thou shalt not make unto thee any graven images, nor serve them.

Thou shalt not take the name of the Lord thy God in vain.

Remember to keep holy the Sabbath day.

Honor thy father and thy mother.

Thou shalt not kill.

Thou shalt not commit adultery.

Thou shalt not steal.

Thou shalt not bear false witness against thy neighbor.

Thou shalt not covet thy neighbor's wife nor goods.

Throughout the ages, people have interpreted and reinterpreted the commandments given by God to Moses until they barely resemble what was given in the first place. They should read:

I am the Lord thy God. Respect my name in all matters.

Do not make a graven image in my likeness and adore it.

Do not use my name in vain.

Remember to keep holy the ground you walk on.

Honor the memory of all who have come before you.

Take not the life of another.

Hold to commitments between yourself and another.

Take not what belongs to another.

Speak truthfully.

Covet not another's spouse nor goods.

The time has come for all to recognize that the laws of the land and the laws of God in respect to life on earth are to be honored. When they are not, someone suffers. Others come to their defense and, seemingly, without mercy, in order to remind the offender that he or she has broken the law. Regrettably, innocents are, at times, caught up in the process.

50

How can differences in the matter of faith be reconciled?

Faith is splintered in the world today. One believes one way and another believes another way. Very few can agree on matters of faith.

To bring about reconciliation would take a monumental effort on the part of all concerned 'to lay on the table' what it is they believe. From there, a sorting out of all differences could result in what is agreed upon. It would not take long to see that most differences are personality and geographical in nature. It would be seen that many ideologies have surfaced from differences in culture.

To bring all under one umbrella is the intention of these pages. First of all, a clarification of the thought process in creation is presented. That alone can stir one's mind to understand the why and wherefore of his present situation.

Next is a way to live in the thought process in order to maintain oneness with it, and finally, how to show the way back to those who stray.

51

How can I get answers?

First of all, you will need to understand that everything originates with the Source of All That Is or God. His thoughts for you are your thoughts, His sight for you is your sight, His words for you are your words, and His actions for you are your actions. But, with this, He also gives you free will to allow this to happen or to go your own way.

In letting God be you, you are letting Him live through you in a way He wants to live through you. He lives through each one of His creations in one way or another, if allowed. It is one grand internet, far vaster than could ever be imagined by man. A person with questions can receive answers by asking others, all the while knowing that the answers are coming from God living through them. Complications set in when the people asked are ones who have gone their own way instead of allowing God to be who they are . . . and the answers are not always correct.

Guardian angels are always available to fill in under the latter circumstances, when the words of others in the world cannot be trusted. This is how they keep a line of communications open between you and God. They are conduits for answers that God should be able to give you through other people. However, angels are available only under certain circumstances. The ones questioning must be living good, gentle, kind and loving lives in everything they do or think or say. Then angels will answer. If ones questioning do not live lives of goodness, gentleness, kindness and love, the answers received will come from other than angels and are not always reliable.

A life on earth can be lived in Oneness with God without reaching out to others for answers or talking with angels. And how that can be done is by living a life of goodness, gentleness, kindness and love and allowing God to live through you in everything you do, or think, or say. God's thoughts for you will be your thoughts, God's sight for you will be your sight, God's words for you will be your words and God's actions for you will be your actions. Answers to all your questions are available in this way.

52

How can I find an avenue to new ways of doing things?

As you go along in life, you often come across avenues that lead to new ways of doing things. Keep an open mind. That way you will remain abreast of advancements in all areas of life. At the present time, man has put a man on the moon, walked in space and made great strides in capturing the essence of the universes. And the future holds promises of much more to come.

Revelations of change come to mind first, then materialize. That is how inventions come about. The revelations are thoughts of inspiration from God. However, God cannot enter the mind of someone whose thoughts are adverse to His way of thinking. They come to those of like mind, meaning ones who are good, gentle, kind and loving and avoid the seven deadly sins

Join your thinking with God's way of thinking. Welcome thoughts of inspiration. The resulting revelations are out of this world!

53

How can I feel fulfilled?

The world, as it is seen today, is a sorry place in which to live. Everyone is trying to do his or her best, but, all too often, falling short of the mark.

The answer is not as might be expected. It is not in the material things of life. Look around, and you will see that material things alone do not bring happiness.

The answer is in self-fulfillment. Self-fulfillment is in doing what comes naturally, nothing else. Doing otherwise leaves no room for self-fulfillment. Doing otherwise only leaves one void of true happiness.

Give a child the chance to look around at the world from different angles, without pressuring him or her to choose a particular course of action. Nine out of ten times, if given the chance, he or she will choose a life of self-fulfillment.

54

What price do I pay for wanting more than God provides for my well-being?

The price you pay is separation from the Mind of God, the Source of all your needs in life. Greed denies all that is rightfully yours. It leaves you scrimping and scraping for bare essentials.

God has an intention for each one of his creations and provides the wherewithal to carry it out. All you have to do is follow through on your intention and allow the wherewithal to flow. The crux of the matter is most people are not aware of God's intention for them. It was there when they were born, but through living a life of separation from the Mind of God, they lost awareness of it.

It cannot be stressed enough that what lies at the bottom of all misfortune in life is a non-alignment of man's mind with the Mind of God. A realignment can be spontaneous. All one need do is be good, gentle, kind and loving and avoid the seven deadly sins of anger, avarice (greed), envy, gluttony, lust, pride, sloth.

55

What was everyday life like on earth before the fall?

First of all, there was no need for sleep; days and nights were the same. There was bliss, which is just as present today as it was then. God created the world in His Love and that Love has not gone anywhere. It is bliss. Very few souls, in body in the world today, take advantage of living in it.

God created each soul of earth with a particular intention in mind. And, in living through each of His creations, He could coalesce a reason for their existence on earth. It was simple. It was to give Him an opportunity to add an avenue of influence from the world to the rest of His creations throughout the universes. The influence of earth is charity.

Each soul of earth lived in this common interest. They understood. Life was the same as it is today, but without bodies. They didn't need e-mail; they had mental telepathy. All realized they were the same; there was no need for 'getting ahead in the world.' Because of their Oneness with 'All That Is,' they knew all they needed to know; there was no need for schools and churches. It was paradise.

Angels wander the universes for various reasons; whereas, souls stay with the globe to which they have been created. Souls of earth wonder what in the world there would be to do in spirit. Souls in spirit wonder what in the world people in bodies are doing running around making and remaking the world to their liking, with no rhyme or reason.

56

What does everyday life mean?

So many things are referred to as everyday life. What does that mean? Some things are even passed off as of no consequence because they are considered just everyday life.

Everyday life is a day in time. It has consequence; therefore, it is important. How it is filled will determine not only the outcome of the immediate life, but also the outcome of the earth and, in turn, the universes. A moment of life is not isolated in time, because time is cohesive.

So, how you spend your life is important. All the nuances that seem like just everyday life add up. Think of it as contributing to posterity. New things, like inventions, make the news, but each and every thought, word and deed of each and every person contributes to the amalgamation of thought patterns throughout eternity. All is affected.

57

How to live everyday life?

On one level, the everyday life of one person is different from the everyday life of another. On another level, they are the same, or can be the same.

Each person has a different agenda and that is why life for one is different from life for another. On another level, lives can be on a common level, where life is led in Oneness with the God consciousness or of One Mind with God. Some have retained that level; others have not. They have led lives that separated them from Oneness with the Mind of God.

From the time of birth until about seven years of age (commonly known as the age of reason), most live in union with God, but later on, after exposure to the world at large, they become lost. Their minds become saturated with distractions that take them away from the one way of thinking.

A return to the state of being of One Mind with God is simple. All one need do is be good, gentle, kind and loving and avoid the seven deadly sins of anger, avarice (greed), envy, gluttony, lust, pride and sloth. The reason they are called deadly is because those who entertain them are dead to God. God knows only Love. He does not know a mind that is otherwise.

58

What is happiness?

Happiness is a state of mind. It is the result of living a life whereby the mind is of One Mind with the Mind of God. Let yourself venture into this state of happiness. It is lasting, not just for the moment but for every moment of your life. When in this state, you enjoy a life that is everlasting.

Happiness is elusive only because those of the world look at it that way. When they look at it otherwise, as something to be enjoyed all the time, that is when they will be of One Mind with the Mind of God. Be the one to demonstrate that this is possible. At first, those in your surroundings will wonder what happened to you. But it won't be long until they will want to enjoy the same kind of life. It is easy. All you need do is let it happen.

Happiness is part of God's makeup. He cannot be otherwise. So if you are created by God, out of his own makeup or radiance, it only stands to reason that your intent is to be happy, too. Do not allow yourself to be caught up in a world of unhappiness. It is a world created by those of separate minds from the Mind of God. Decide not to be a part of that world.

59

What does it mean to live a life of fantasy?

God created man to live a life of wonderment or, as you might say, a life of fantasy. Up until the time of the fall, man, in spirit form, did live a life of wonderment. He roamed the world with ease, with no concern about modes of transportation. There was no need.

After the fall, he developed a body, which hindered his traveling with ease. Ever since, he has lived a life of wonderment or fantasy, but it has taken on different proportions. Without body, his view of life was limitless. Now, it is limited.

Man does not realize he continues to live in a world of wonderment or fantasy. When he sees something developed that is beyond what he can conceive of as possible, he calls it an invention. An invention receives applause because it is something that seems unusual. What has happened is the person doing the inventing is someone who has kept an open mind to the Mind of God.

The mind of man in body has the same access to the Mind of God as the mind of man in spirit. Live a life that is gentle, kind and loving, and you will be of One Mind with the Mind of God. Your thoughts will be God's thoughts for you.

60

What is meant by a sound mind in a sound body?

Everything that exists is sound or unsound. Sound is the energy that courses throughout all that exists. It is in wavelengths. And it is good. Maintaining alignment or attunement to it is necessary for good health . . . a sound mind in a sound body.

Soundness of mind comes first. Soundness of body follows automatically. A sound mind is one that is attuned to the Mind of God. An unsound mind is one that is not attuned to the Mind of God. Since God's mind is one of Love only, it follows that to be sound of mind and body, one must live in the Love.

Life is simple. It is man who complicates it. Living a life of goodness, being gentle, kind and loving each and every moment of each and every day, keeps one in tune with the sound of the universes. When that happens, one is living in the God consciousness, the cosmic consciousness, the universal consciousness, the All That Is.

61

What is disease?

The word disease is pronounced with the accent on the second syllable, whereas it was originally pronounced with the accent on the first syllable. The latter pronunciation is descriptive of the meaning of the word.

Not many look at disease as a lack of ease, but that is what it is, no matter what type. In a healthy body, all organs function synchronically. In an unhealthy body, they do not. A body retains its healthy state when nothing disturbs it. Lack of ease disturbs it. Lack of ease can disturb a body in three ways. A disease that manifests as a weakening of tissue, such as cancer, is caused by a giving-up attitude. The person looks on life as hopeless. A feeling of restriction causes a disease that manifests as excessive such as breathing too hard (asthma) or body growth (nodules, warts, etc.). The person feels bound in some way. A disease that manifests as a nervous condition, such as MS, Alzheimer's,

Parkinson's, is caused by stress. The person tries but cannot cope with life.

Love is the key. Living a life that is gentle, kind and loving nullifies lack of ease and keeps a body healthy.

62

How can I live a life of ease?

A life of ease is usually thought of as one that includes a big house, lots of money and a general feeling of "having it all." Those who have all this are envied. They are looked to as ones that should be emulated. They are often looked to as the ultimate of success.

A life of ease is one where a person lives a life in harmony with the sound of the universes, on a wavelength that synchronizes with All That Is . . . the spirit of God. It is a life of ease because it is easy. All one need do is realize what it is that makes the difference between a life of ease and one of dis-ease.

The sound of the universes is a consciousness. It is the God consciousness. It is within this consciousness that life exists. It is within this consciousness that life is easy. No matter where you are, you experience a oneness with it. All is good and gentle, kind and loving.

A separation from this consciousness is what results in a life of dis-ease. It is a turning away from a life of being good and gentle, kind and loving. It is a dying to the spirit of God. It is the entertainment of what are called the seven deadly sins . . . anger, avarice (greed), envy, gluttony, lust, pride and sloth.

Living a simple life, a life of ease, is living a good and gentle, kind and loving life in the spirit of God.

63

Why do bodies age?

Aging is a process that begins at birth and signifies withdrawal of a soul from life in body. The body is mortal, meaning it has a life span; whereas, the soul is immortal, meaning it lives forever.

In the beginning, souls were in spirit only. This lasted until the fall of man. It was then that the fallen angel Lucifer tempted one named Adam to want more than God was providing for what he was doing. This was impossible to grant, because in creating, God includes all that is necessary for the well-being and survival of a particular creation. Nothing can be added or taken away later.

Souls, but not all, followed Adam in his falling away from God. Bodies formed. They were meant to be temporary coverings until the souls returned to their oneness with God. Until this day, some of these same souls have not returned. They stay in their earthbound mentality and are born again and again, without returning to the Light.

While this is going on, souls who remained in spirit and one with God take on bodies to reach and remind the lost souls of what they need to do to return to the Light. But what happens is many of the souls who come to save get caught up in the ways of the lost souls and become lost themselves. When the souls who come to save stay in the Light and the lost souls listen to them, there will be no further need for bodies.

64

How does a good gene become a bad gene in the process of heredity?

The word gene is a code word for the unit in the body that carries hereditary characteristics. When God created the body to house the separate soul, he introduced characteristics that would be regenerated from lifetime to lifetime. In other words, they would be inherited.

As time went by, the characteristics of genes were disturbed by the introduction of animal genes into the procreative process. This happened through cohabitation between humans and animals. When animal extremities occurred in newborns, they were cut off. People were advised not to marry another who might have animal genes. To this day, the admonition continues, but the advisement is against marrying cousins unless thrice removed.

The thought process also affects the function of genetic codes. What a man believes in his heart, so shall he become.

To this day, abnormalities in the body are attributed to 'the sins of the fathers.' For instance, if you believe hard enough and long enough a certain way, the genetic code complies with your way of thinking. However, a reversal of the process can happen if a person reintroduces purity of thought; that is, becomes good, gentle, kind and loving and avoids the seven deadly sins.

65

What are roads to recovery?

Roads to recovery describe roads people can travel to be free of whatever is holding them back from enjoying perfect health.

First of all, comfort & relaxation are necessary before a person can lift his or her sights beyond what is being experienced. Many means to that end are available, such as relaxation exercises, massage, chiropractic, etc. Proper diet is another. And a job and a roof over one's head is another.

Reasons for chronic poor health are many, but usually fall into the following categories:

1. Weakening of tissue, such as cancer, which is caused by a giving-up attitude. The person looks on life as hopeless.

2. Excess, such as breathing too hard (asthma) or body growth (nodules, warts, acne, etc.) which is caused by a feeling of restriction. The person feels bound in some way.

3. Nervousness, such as MS, Alzheimer's, Parkinson's, which is caused by stress. The person tries but cannot cope with life.

4. Heredity.

5. Environment.

6. Possession

The first three on the list are usually referred to as disease, and are usually pronounced with the accent on the second syllable instead of the first, as originally intended. When it is realized that the disease is because of a lack of ease (dis-ease), a person can take steps to isolate root causes and expunge them.

Hereditary malfunctions are the result of dysfunctional genes inherited from ancestors who lived lives that injected discordant notes (through unsound lives that they led) into the soundness of hereditary codes.

Environmental causes can be rectified by talking to those who perpetuate them. Air breathed and food eaten should be as pure as possible.

Possession by an interfering spirit can be at the root of dis-ease and/or afflictions present as forerunners to future malfunctioning of genetic codes.

66

What is spiritual healing therapy?

Healing happens on a mental level. What happens on a physical level is the result of healing on a mental level. Physical therapy and ingestion of supplements as a means of healing are of no value in the process of healing on a mental level. The only thing they do is relax and nourish a person so that the person is ready to be healed on a mental level.

Stressing relaxation and/or supplements as a means toward healing confuses a person. A dependency develops that supersedes a change in mental attitudes. "If I do this or take that, I will be well" is the usual approach to change. Some spend a lifetime in this rut, always looking for healing that is never going to happen.

All that is necessary, on a physical level, is a few simple limbering exercises and the eating of fruits, vegetables, nuts and grains. No more. Supplements may be nourishing, but they are an added, unnecessary expense. On the mental level, all that is necessary is an introduction to a life of goodness, gentleness, kindness and love. The result is a life of ease that displaces disease.

67

What happens in decomposition of the body?

The reason for keeping bodies at least three days is that is how long it takes for the body to decompose. When a body is buried before that length of time, the decomposition process is delayed.

The body is a vessel used by the soul while in earthly incarnation. When spirit leaves, the body starts to decompose. And while decomposing, it lets off a stench usually associated with rotting matter. When you are around someone who has just died, you will notice a pleasing aroma. That emanates from the spirit that is leaving the body.

Burying a body before three days have elapsed interrupts the natural process of decomposition. You may wonder why it matters. It matters because burying a body before three days contaminates the ingredients of the soil and slows rejuvenation of the soil for further use. That is the reason why bodies are buried in protective boxes. It is not to protect the body, but to protect the soil.

Embalming does not interfere with the decomposition process. And cremation is not wrong. It just interrupts the natural order of life.

68

Will there ever be peace in the world?

There will be peace in the world when everybody understands what caused loss of peace in the first place, and then does something about it.

In the beginning, the world was a very peaceful place in which to live. It was beautiful. But then avarice (greed) set in. It originated with Lucifer, the angel who had fallen out with God because he wanted more than God was providing for what he was doing. And who, in turn, tempted the one we know as Adam to do the same thing. Adam went along with the idea and that was the end of peace in the world. Greed is not part of God's way of thinking. It is called a deadly sin, because the person who entertains such a thought is dead to God's way of thinking.

God's thoughts are loving thoughts only. For peace to return to the world, everyone's thoughts will have to return to loving thoughts only.

69

Is the world going through a cleansing?

Something is going on all over the world, and it is a puzzle to its inhabitants. The phenomenon is not an environmental problem, as many suppose. It is much more. It is a world cleansing.

The world has reached that stage in its existence when it needs a monumental bath. Filth is piling up, out of all proportions. Wars have left debris over most of the earth, in one form or another, above and below ground. Pollutants have filled the atmosphere until very little clean air exists.

Cleansing of the world started around 2,000 years ago. It was a time when an alignment of the stars and planets let the Light from the Godhead, or Source of all things, reach earth in its fullest intensity. The Light has been cleansing earth of impurities ever since, and will continue to do so until further realignment of the stars and planets.

Peaking of the Light will take place around 2011. By then, impurities will be gone. The earth will be pure again. Then the Light will wane. Once before, in the existence of the world, a cleansing took place. It was at the time of the great flood, when dinosaurs disappeared from the face of the earth.

70

Should people take it seriously when there is an earthquake?

They should take it much more seriously than they do. The world is falling apart before their very eyes. And they are helpless to do anything about it.

The number of earthquakes can gauge the life of a planet. The planet cannot go on forever breaking up into pieces, a little here, a little there. That is what happened to the planet between Mars and Jupiter until it fell apart completely. Its pieces continue to rotate in the same path that the whole planet did.

All of God's creations are brought into being in Love. And they are sustained in Love. When that Love dies, the creation can no longer sustain itself. It breaks up and dies. This is what is happening to planet Earth. The Love has been dying ever since the fall of man . . . and continues to die.

71

What causes the earth to wobble?

When the world was new, the wind blew in only one direction, and that was in a circle around the globe. Now the wind blows in four different directions, north and south and east and west. This change in pattern came about as the earth aged. The earth needed more support than the wind provided in blowing in only one direction. It is something that is little known and is the cause of much havoc in the earth's weather systems. It is known by science, but just not spoken of much.

Imagine a ball that is steady on a pedestal and then imagine a breeze blowing around it in one direction. Now imagine the same ball with a breeze blowing around it in four different directions. Do you see the difference that would make in the ball's steadiness?

Now imagine the world with the wind blowing around it in a circle. Then imagine it with the wind blowing around it in four different directions. Can you see now how weather patterns can be unpredictable?

When the world turns on its axis, it wobbles. This is the cause of it.

72

Where is Atlantis?

Atlantis is a name given to part of a continent that disappeared during a flooding incident, but not at the time of the great flood so often spoken of. It is now called a subcontinent. Many fantasies have developed from the interest paid to the time of Atlantis. Most of them are just that.

Atlantis had become corrupt beyond all human imagination. What is going on in the world today would not come anywhere near. In the flooding, which was a cleansing process, its connection to a continent weakened and, as a result, it disappeared beneath the waters.

It could be found in the area of what is called the Bermuda triangle. That is the reason for happenings in that area. If man watched the regularity of happenings in that region, he could be more aware of the next one, and steer clear. Even after all these years since the flooding, a pulsar still exists.

Its purpose was to monitor stellar happenings. In its cyclic performance, a ray of energy crosses paths with surface and air, and even underwater objects, and sets them into a spin and eventual loss.

73

Are we in "the end times"?

Yes. There have already been changes that people do not recognize as the beginning of the end. They are numerous. To name a few, there have been plagues, drought, famine, earthquakes, hurricanes and tornadoes. They will become even more numerous as time goes by.

The Creator of the universes brings his creations into being with Love. When Love dies, the creation can no longer sustain itself. And that is what is happening to the world. It happened to the planet between Mars and Jupiter. It broke up. It is now in the form of what is called the asteroid belt. The same thing will happen to the world. Love has diminished to the point where the world can no longer sustain itself.

Those living during 'the end times' will have an option of staying with the world during its final throes or rising in the rapture. Spirit discs are hovering for that purpose.

74

How could Jesus predict that 144,000 would rise in the rapture?

He knew an approximate number of 144,000. God's knowing, and hence Jesus', was based on the condition of the world at the time and the minds of the people, in spirit and in body. Such a large assessment seems beyond the scope of human comprehension, and it is. God's knowing is a summarization, something like the way a computer works. All the facts are registered, as they go, and the click of a key brings up a total. It was easy for Jesus to see the approximate number who would make it.

75

Are little children included in that number?

The number 144,000 applies to all those who have reached the age of reason and are living in God's Love. Children who have not reached the age of reason will be brought along. Children, whose caregivers are not part of the 144,000, will stay on earth, but, as the earth disintegrates and souls are in spirit only, the innocent children will soon realize their places on the seven planes of spirit. Those who have reached the age of reason and are not in God's Love will wander the world until the final judgment.

76

Will angels who have incarnated in body be part of the 144,000?

No. When they leave body, they will go directly into space on what could be called a space disk, just as they do now when leaving. If they have forgotten who they are, memory will be restored to them immediately. None will return to the formless state.

77

Who is the anti-christ?

Anti-Christ is a word used to describe a personage who will supposedly appear during the end times to set the world aright in regard to what it believes about Jesus.

The personage has appeared many times in the form of those who oppose the teachings of Jesus. The personage is Lucifer, the fallen angel. He and his followers have been banished from the world by Archangel Michael, but his influence lives on in a legacy of anti-christ publications.

78

What is outer space and who is there?

Outer space is a place occupied by numerous stars and planets, orbiting in their designated patterns. Some stars and planets have inhabitants. Others do not. The inhabitants are in spirit form, except for those of earth, who have bodies. The inhabitants stay with the star or planet in which they were created. They are referred to as souls.

Traveling freely throughout the universes are angels. They are so busy they do not have what might be called home bases. If they are not associated with one star or planet, they are associated with another. Some angels are assigned to be guardian angels of lights born into bodies on earth.

If a trip is a long one, angels may use what is known to man as a spaceship or UFO (unidentified flying object). The ships, which are of various sizes, are in spirit form but, sometimes, can be seen by humans who have eyes to see. At other times, they manifest on a dimension that can be seen by more people. Besides conveying angels throughout the universes, spaceships can be ridden by those in body form. These trips are usually short. Sometimes a person is anesthetized so that the experience is not fearful. Those not fearful experience a ride to the fullest. Some who have been on trips speak of operations, etc. They are conducted on a spirit level and do no harm to the body.

Souls created to stay with planets are all of the same degree of Light. Angels, depending on what they were created to do, are of different degrees of Light.

Printed in Great Britain
by Amazon